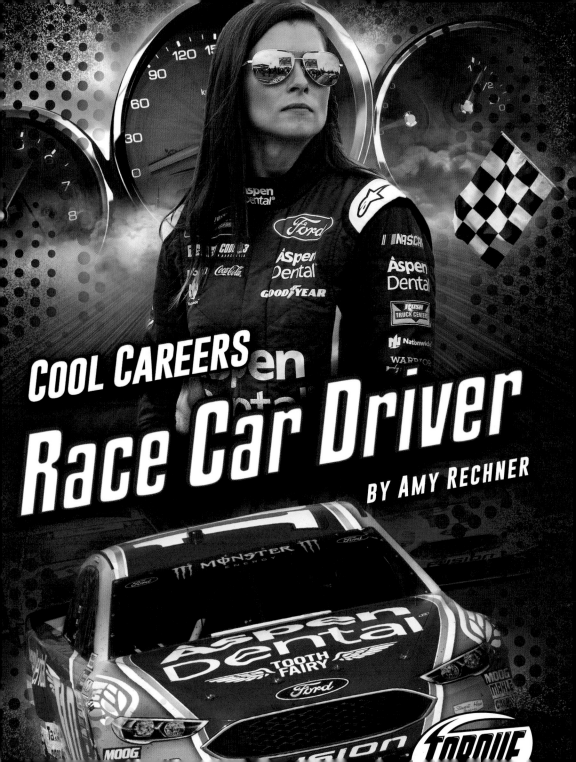

COOL CAREERS

Race Car Driver

BY AMY RECHNER

Are you ready to take it to the extreme?
Torque books thrust you into the action-packed world
of sports, vehicles, mystery, and adventure. These books may
include dirt, smoke, fire, and dangerous stunts.
WARNING: read at your own risk.

This edition first published in 2020 by Bellwether Media, Inc.

No part of this publication may be reproduced in whole or in part without written permission of the publisher.
For information regarding permission, write to Bellwether Media, Inc., Attention: Permissions Department,
6012 Blue Circle Drive, Minnetonka, MN 55343.

Library of Congress Cataloging-in-Publication Data

LC record for Race Car Driver available at https://lccn.loc.gov/2018061464

TABLE OF CONTENTS

Race Ready................................4

In the Driver's Seat 6

Team Effort............................10

Driving Skills 14

Someone with Drive...................18

Glossary............................... 22

To Learn More 23

Index 24

Race Ready

It is almost race time. The **pit** crew checks every inch of the race car. The driver puts on his helmet and climbs into the seat. The loudspeaker calls, "Drivers, start your engines!"

The driver pulls up to his starting position on the track. The green flag waves. The engine roars. The car is off!

FAST FIXER

A Formula One pit crew once changed a car's four tires in less than two seconds!

In the Driver's Seat

Race car drivers are the public face of a racing team. They drive specially built cars in different events.

Races can cover long distances. Drivers must stay focused the whole time! Some drivers race around large oval tracks. Others compete in road races that go through cities.

road race

A LONG DRIVE

Many NASCAR races are 500 miles (805 kilometers) long. That is 200 laps around the track! These races can take more than three hours to finish.

karts

Many kids discover the thrill of racing with karts. They learn basic driving skills as young as age 5. A lot of famous race car drivers started with karts.

Many drivers use kart racing to train for open-wheel racing, like **Formula One**. Others move on to stock car racing. They hope to race with **NASCAR** someday!

Kinds of Racing

STOCK CAR RACING

- CARS: MODIFIED STREET CARS
- RACES: LAPS AROUND A TRACK
- MAJOR RACING GROUP: NASCAR

OPEN-WHEEL RACING

- CARS: ONE SEAT, NO TOP, WHEELS OUTSIDE
- RACES: TRACKS AND ROAD COURSES
- MAJOR RACING GROUPS: INDYCAR, FORMULA ONE

DRAG RACING

- CARS: MODIFIED STREET CARS, DRAGSTERS
- RACES: SHORT, STRAIGHT DISTANCES
- MAJOR RACING GROUP: NATIONAL HOT ROD ASSOCIATION

RALLY CAR RACING

- CARS: MODIFIED STREET CARS
- RACES: CLOSED-OFF ROADS
- MAJOR RACING GROUPS: INTERNATIONAL AUTOMOBILE FEDERATION, RALLY AMERICA

Team Effort

Drivers cannot do their jobs without support. Racing teams must find **sponsors** to pay for the car and other expenses. The sponsor's name decorates all of the driver's gear, from the car to the driver's racing suit and helmet!

On race day, more than a dozen **mechanics** and **engineers** get the car ready. A small pit crew stands by to switch out tires and refuel.

pit crew

Race Day Checklist

- ☑ **7:00 AM: ARRIVE AT GARAGE FOR CAR INSPECTION**

- ☑ **10:45 AM: GO OVER DRIVING PLAN WITH CREW**

- ☑ **12:45 PM: HEAD TO THE STARTING POSITION**

- ☑ **1:30 PM: RACE TIME!**

- ☑ **4:45 PM: CROSS THE FINISH LINE!**

- ☑ **5:15 PM: MAKE NOTES ON HOW THE RACE WENT**

- ☑ **6:30 PM: TALK TO FANS AND REPORTERS**

- ☑ **8:00 PM: DINNER WITH SPONSORS**

Between races, drivers work closely with their team to improve the cars. Drivers sense the tiniest changes in the way a car runs. They spend long hours before and after races going over the cars with the team.

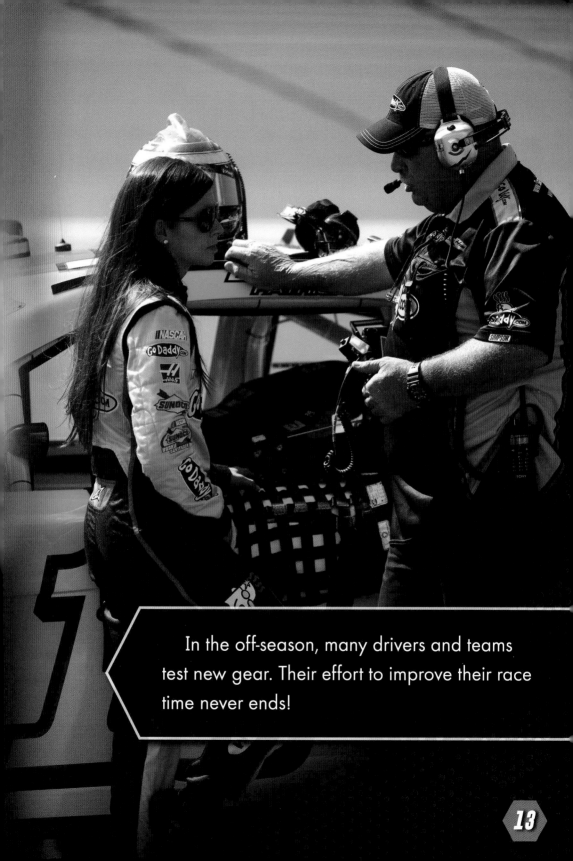

In the off-season, many drivers and teams test new gear. Their effort to improve their race time never ends!

Driving Skills

Race car drivers must be fit and strong. Breathing is harder at high speeds! Drivers work out to build strong lungs. They must have strong muscles to be stable around turns.

Drivers must also stay alert. It is easy to crash! Drivers watch for different colored flags that tell them what is happening around the track. The crew chief tells them about dangers through their headsets.

An important part of a driver's job is speaking with reporters and fans. Drivers must have good manners and be comfortable talking to people.

Drivers also appear at special events for the sponsors. Many drivers use their fame to help **charities** raise money. Some even start their own charities!

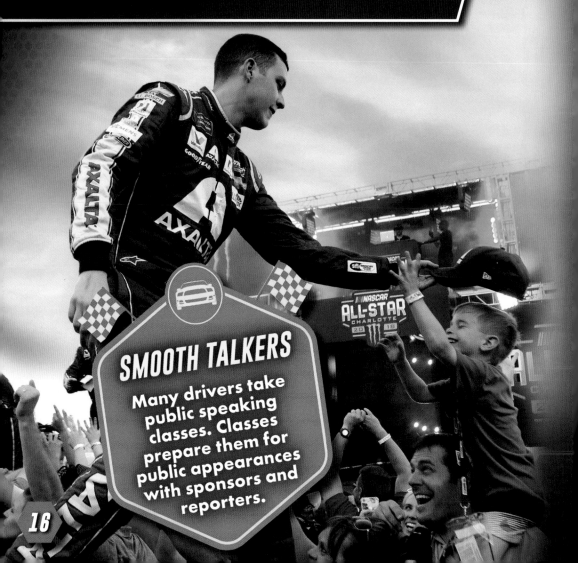

SMOOTH TALKERS

Many drivers take public speaking classes. Classes prepare them for public appearances with sponsors and reporters.

Erik Jones

BORN: MAY 30, 1996

HOMETOWN: BYRON, MICHIGAN

EDUCATION: SWARTZ CREEK ACADEMY

PREVIOUS EXPERIENCE:
- STARTED RACING AT AGE 7 IN QUARTER MIDGET CARS
- BEGAN STOCK CARS AT AGE 13

ACHIEVEMENTS:
- FIRST DRIVER TO BE NAMED ROOKIE OF THE YEAR FOR THREE MAJOR NASCAR SERIES IN 2015, 2016, AND 2017
- YOUNGEST CHAMPION OF THE NASCAR CAMPING WORLD TRUCK SERIES (2015) AT AGE 19

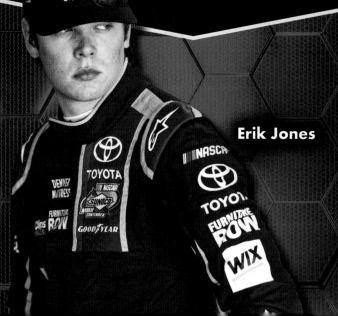

Erik Jones

Someone with Drive

midget cars

Many drivers start their racing **careers** with karts or small **midget cars**. They practice racing on local tracks. Young hopefuls can buy a pit pass to meet racing teams and pit crews.

Some racing schools teach special skills to students over age 14. Some **professional** drivers even start racing through video games!

Career Path

KARTING

MIDGET CAR RACING

JOIN LOCAL RACING ORGANIZATION

GET A COMPETITION LICENSE

FIND SPONSORS AND TEAM

TRY OUT BIGGER RACES!

An important step for any driver is joining an **amateur** racing club. These clubs set up local races. They often offer classes and help drivers meet sponsors.

Racing clubs help drivers earn their **competition license**. Then drivers can start racing as professionals. Flags up!

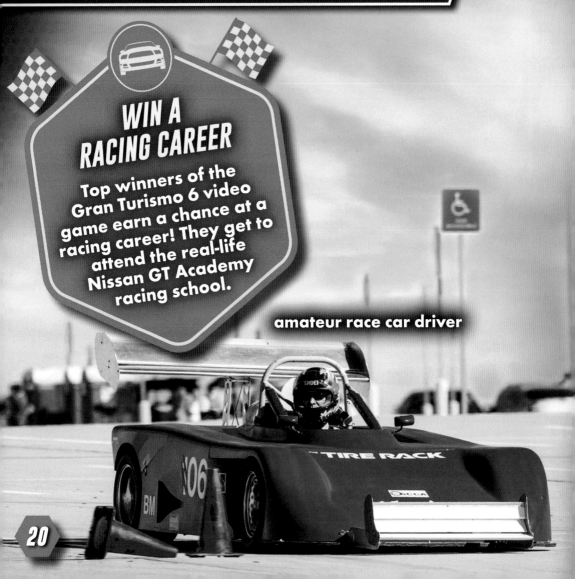

WIN A RACING CAREER

Top winners of the Gran Turismo 6 video game earn a chance at a racing career! They get to attend the real-life Nissan GT Academy racing school.

amateur race car driver

Race Car Driver Wanted!

SEEKING A SUCCESSFUL AMATEUR DRIVER READY TO TAKE THEIR CAREER TO THE NEXT LEVEL!

EDUCATION: HIGH SCHOOL DIPLOMA; COLLEGE DEGREE IS HELPFUL

EXPERIENCE: KARTS, LOCAL RACETRACK; KNOWLEDGE OF AUTO MECHANICS A MUST

QUALITIES:
- FAST AND FEARLESS
- FRIENDLY AND POLITE
- STRONG AND FIT
- CALM UNDER PRESSURE

SALARIES FOR THIS POSITION CAN REACH $22 MILLION!

Glossary

amateur—a person who does something for fun and not as a job

careers—jobs people do for a long time

charities—organizations that help people in need

competition license—an official document that gives a driver permission to race

engineers—people who design and build race cars and other machines

Formula One—an international type of open-wheel car racing

mechanics—people who fix machines and engines so they run properly

midget cars—very small race cars with powerful engines

NASCAR—National Association for Stock Car Auto Racing; NASCAR organizes stock car races in the United States.

pit—the area next to the track where cars stop for service during a race

professional—a driver or team that makes money racing cars

sponsors—people or organizations that pay the cost of an activity or event

To Learn More

AT THE LIBRARY

Adamson, Thomas K. *Stock Cars*. Minneapolis, Minn.: Bellwether Media, 2019.

Fishman, Jon M. *Danica Patrick*. Minneapolis, Minn.: Lerner Publications, 2018.

Nagelhout, Ryan. *20 Fun Facts About Auto Racing*. New York, N.Y.: Gareth Stevens, 2016.

ON THE WEB

FACTSURFER

Factsurfer.com gives you a safe, fun way to find more information.

1. Go to www.factsurfer.com.

2. Enter "race car driver" into the search box and click Q.

3. Select your book cover to see a list of related web sites.

Index

career path, 19

careers, 18, 20

cars, 4, 5, 6, 10, 12

charities, 16

competition license, 20

crew chief, 15

engineers, 10

flag, 5, 15, 20

Formula One, 5, 8, 9

gear, 4, 10, 13, 15

Gran Turismo, 20

job posting, 21

Jones, Erik, 17

karts, 8, 18

kinds of racing, 9

mechanics, 10

midget cars, 18

NASCAR, 7, 8, 9

Nissan GT Academy, 20

off-season, 13

open-wheel racing, 8, 9

pit crew, 4, 5, 10, 18

public speaking, 16

race day checklist, 11

racing club, 20

racing schools, 18, 20

racing team, 6, 10, 12, 13, 18

sponsors, 10, 16, 20

stock car racing, 8, 9

track, 5, 7, 15, 18

video games, 18, 20

work out, 14

The images in this book are reproduced through the courtesy of: Action Sports Photography, front cover (hero), pp. 4, 5, 9 (top left), 10, 11 (top middle, bottom middle), 15, 17, 21; action sports, front cover (car), p. 11 (bottom); ZUMA Press, Inc./ Alamy, p. 6; David Wall/ Alamy, p. 7; Jaggat Rashidi, p. 8; Ev. Safronov, pp. 9 (top right), 14; Phillip Rubino, p. 9 (bottom left); Taras Vyshnya, p. 9 (bottom right); Melanie Hoffman, ▮▮▮top); PJF Military Collection/ Alamy, p. 12; Phelan M. Ebenhack/ AP Images, p. 13; Cal Sport Media/ Alamy, p. 16; Daniel Gangur, p. 18; photoStock10, p. 19 ▮▮ left); john j. Klaiber jr, p. 19 (top right, middle left); PRESSLAB, p. 19 (middle right); Matthew Jacques, p. 19 (bottom left); Fabio Pagani, p. 19 (bottom right); Ed Endicott/ Alamy, p. 20.